create a new reality

reflection press

unCommon fruit series

here is an expanded moment · · ·

outside of linear time to pause

...relax with a simple, meditative story with sparse, raw imagery, open to be read on multiple levels.

faces and figures are yours to interpret and embellish. the background is left plain to express not only a sense of eternal space, but also an opportunity for you to draw, color, paint.

create.

know self. play with your thoughts. each moment you will be creating peace.

(BE) With special love for my matthew, my zai and our baby (38)

ISBN 978-0-9843799-4-1

Library of Congress Control Number (LCCN): 2012917945

Join the movement that begins within. Freely decorate your world with peace.

Download "i see peace" mini cards on our website: www.reflectionpress.com/iseepeace

i see, you see, we all see peace!

"create a new reality" ~ www.reflectionpress.com

Reflection Press is an independent publisher of radical children's books and works that expand spiritual and cultural awareness.

We seek to empower effective co-creators in our new reality through materials and services that are always rooted in a sense of playfulness and exuberance and continually promote sourcing trust and knowing within the individual.

peace love trust now peace

i
see
peace
✳

maya gonzalez

what
is
peace?

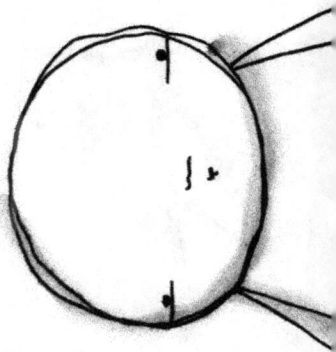

like many things
in life
peace is not
what
i thought
it was.

i was surprised wher

surprised,

because
i had never
felt
anything
like it.

first felt peace.

apparently i had never known
what peace was or
what it felt like.

peace
had been
more of a
concept.

inner peace

but even though
i knew what
it felt like,

harmony

peace was still
hard
to put into
w o r d s.

calm

quiet

freedom from civil disturbance

tranquility

dict-
ion-
ary

peace affects
everything

there is no end to
how deep
it

can

go

peace is infinite.

i have only just begun

i didn't know someone like me
got to have peace.

i have been clumsy in life

but
peace belongs
to everyone.
everyone
can have
peace.

because

peace

begins

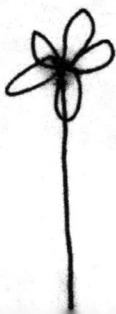

within

how?

when i listen
to myself

(all)

of my thoughts,
my feelings
and intuitions,

i learn to trust
myself

thoughts

feelings

intuitions

and peace begins.

when i can see
all of me
without

j

u

d

g

m

e

n

t

※

peace begins.

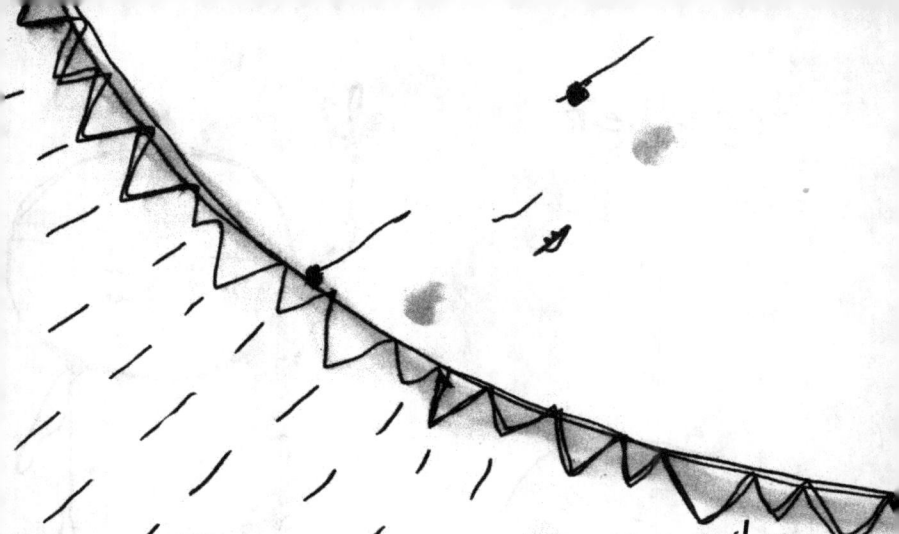

when
i relax
into
life
and go
with the
natural and
creative flow
of my being

this
for me
is peace.

together

we can stand
in peace.

together we can see

everyone's peace is

unique.

together
we can
see

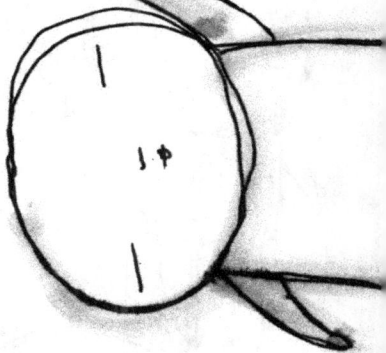

everyone's
peace is
important.

together we can

see a new peace.

but,
what about when we don't
want to be together?

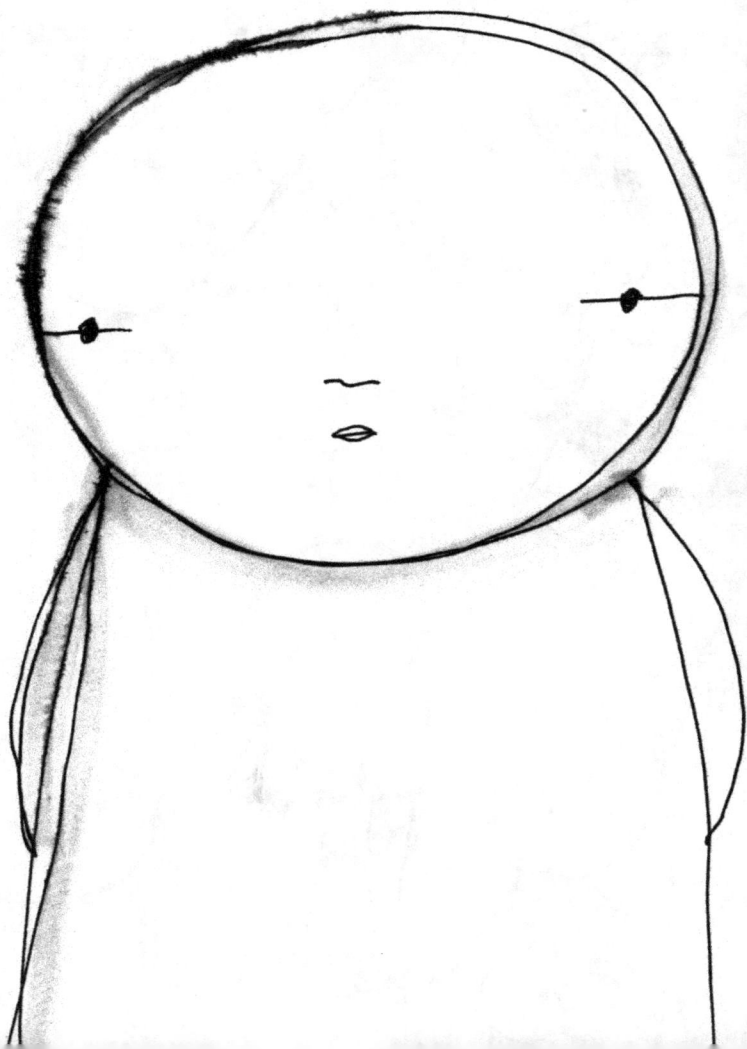

can there still be
peace?

yes.   peace is independent.

we   don't   have   to
we   don't   have   to
we   don't   have   to

agree.

be friends.

like each other.

there can still be
peace between us.

peace is like a
flower. it is
beautiful all
the time

no matter what feeling
is passing through.

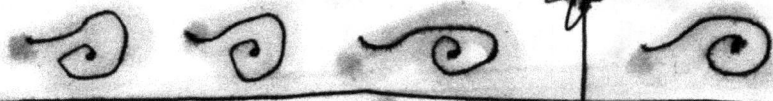

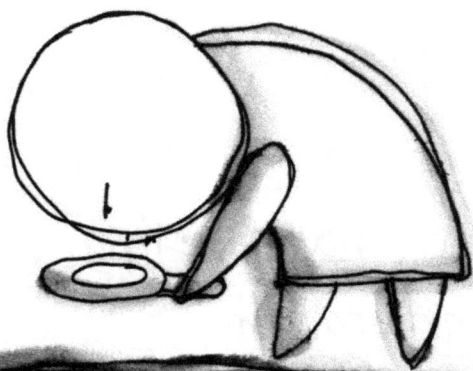

sometimes
peace
is
closer
than
we think.

sometimes
we want to
believe in peace
but it doesn't seem
possible.

but believing that peace is

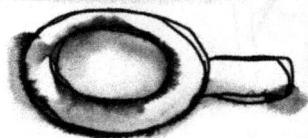

possible is the first step.

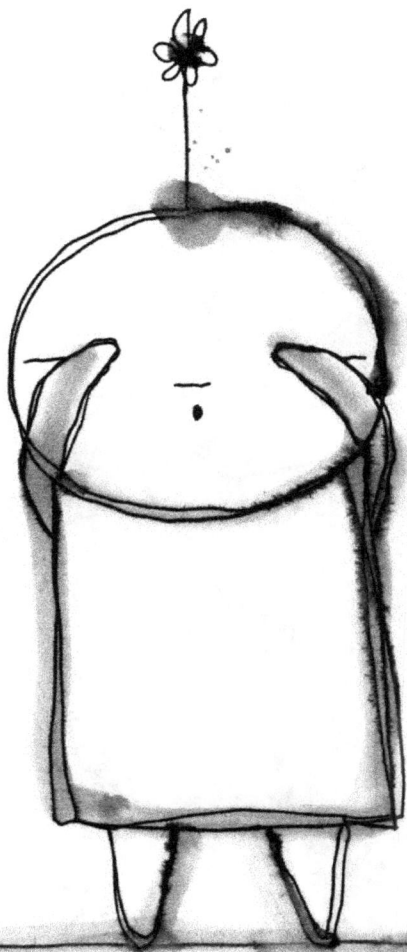

when we believe in something
it is more likely that we
will see it.

believing is seeing.

some people
see
peace
inside

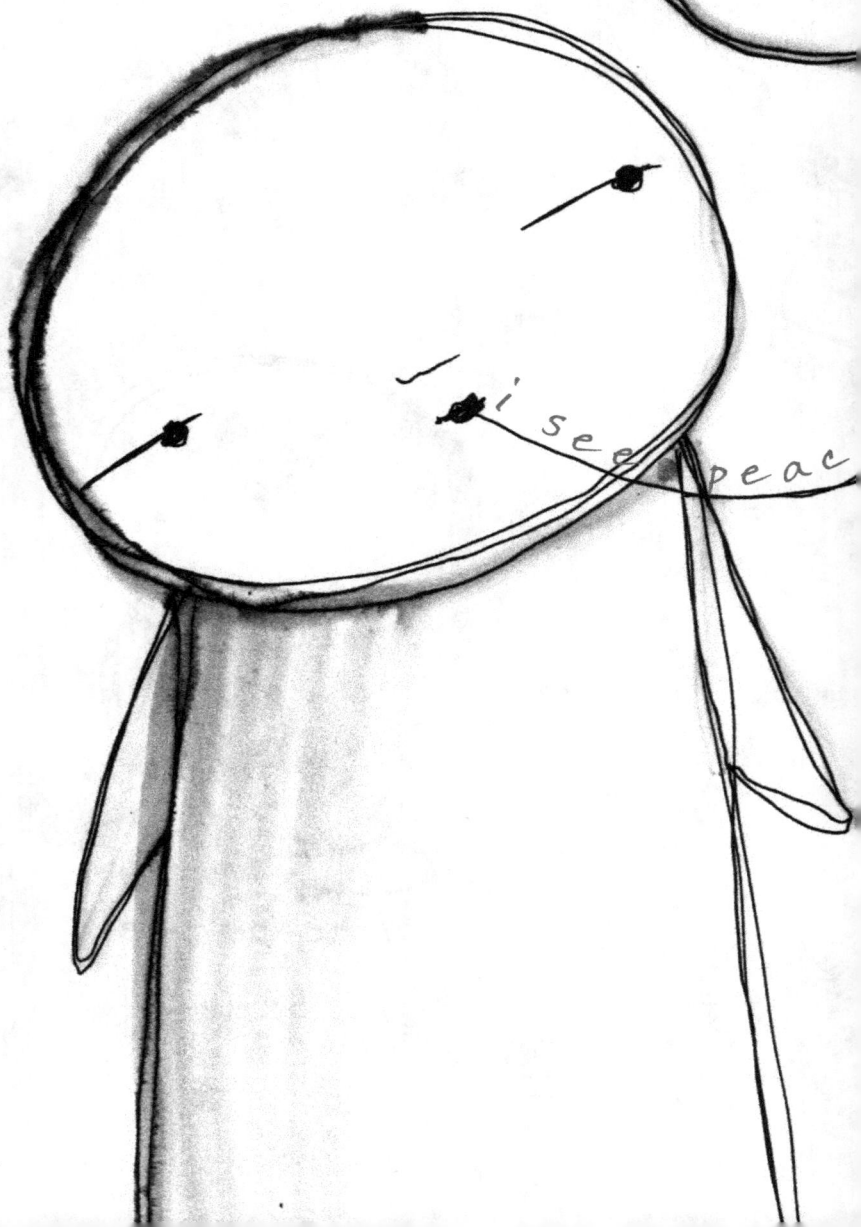

i see peace i see peace i see peace i see peace i see peace i see peace i see peace i see peace i see peace

go about
your day,

and here
and there,

say to
yourself...

i see

peace.

and you will.

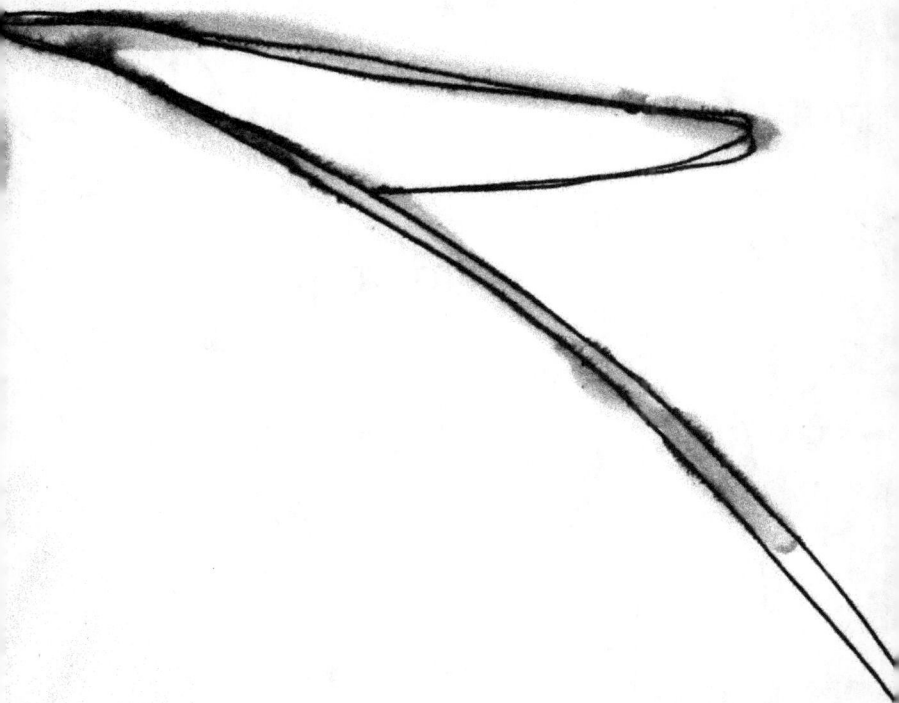

it may be quite small.

but it
is
infinite.

and if you can see it once.

you can see
it again.

and again.

just say the words

i

see

peace

and see.

journal

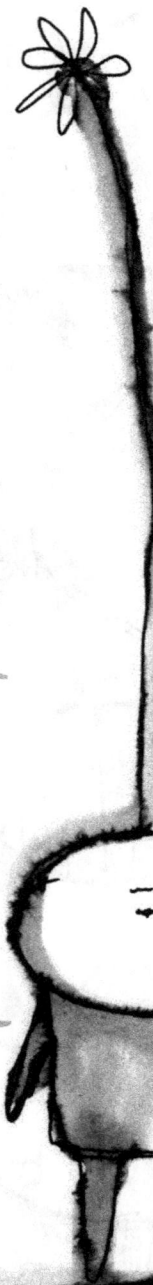

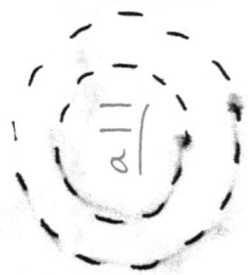

my thoughts
my feelings
my intuitions

my thoughts

my intuitions

my feelings

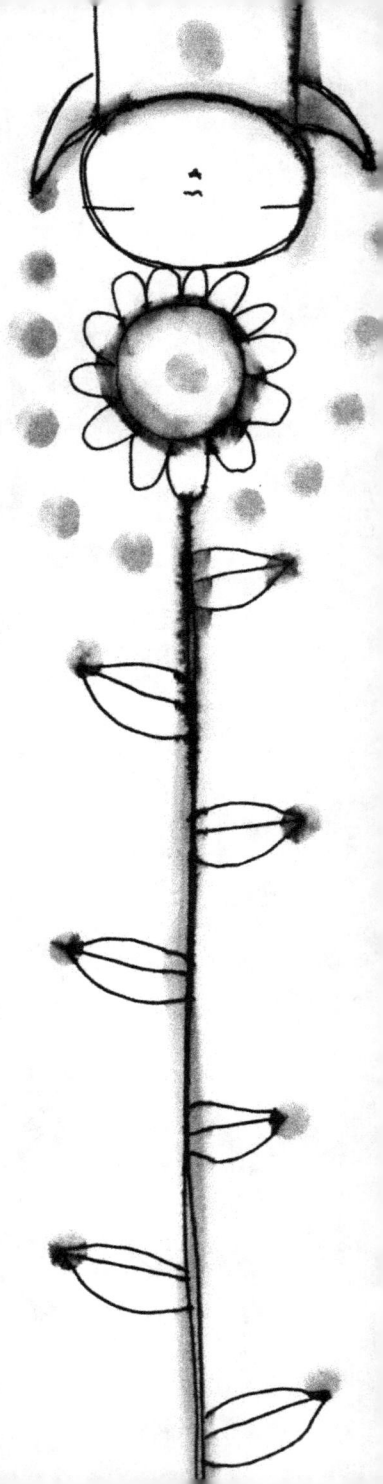

what am i thinking right now?

who i really am

what does peace mean to

me?

ƎƆA Ǝꟼ

the peace i see

the peace i create

the peace i am

WE SEE PEACE

a special thanks to our kickstarter supporters

adelina anthony and marisa becerra
cristina serna
dad & joe
deva luna
gail terman
gary d. page
the grateful chics, joy and claire
harriet rohmer
jamie campbell naidoo
janet del mundo
karen jonsson
karen, kara, & aydin
kitty page
ktern
lesly, geoffrey, and miguel lópez
marta huante robles
mira reisberg
nancy silverrod
pam rieser
roni simone
sarah french
shannan wong
teresa

the story of
FLOWERS

FLOWER POWER

During the tumultuous era of the late 60s and early 70s flowers were used as a symbol of peace in response to the Vietnam War. Allen Ginsberg first wrote about using flowers to "transform war protests into peaceful affirmative spectacles" and affect the "fear, anger and threat that is inherent within protests" in 1965. He encouraged protestors to hand flowers out to policemen, press, politicians and spectators to maintain peace during a particularly challenging demonstration. FLOWER POWER as it became known began in Berkeley, CA. It proved so effective as a symbol and a tool for peace that its use spread across the globe. Imagine that!

about maya

I am an artist, author, educator, co-founder of Reflection Press and peacemaker! Peace has been a far more fascinating and curious journey than my small assumptions could have contained. Peace has made me larger and pleased me no end. My personal peace has been so precious and surprising that my pleasure has spilled out into story and art to express, learn more (always!) and share.

I whisper I SEE PEACE during my hardest moments. And I laugh out I SEE PEACE during my most awesome moments. Peace is always there.

As you play with seeing peace, not only will you change, but our world will change. Thank you for all you do! Every step counts.

You are free to feel as much peace as you dare! You are free to change this world to support someone as distinct and beautiful as YOU!

I see peace in you.

love, maya